20 Ways to Cook

COD

Gail Duff

Thomas Harmsworth Publishing Company

First published in 1994 by
Thomas Harmsworth Publishing
Company
Old Rectory Offices
Stoke Abbott
Beaminster
Dorset DT8 3JT
United Kingdom

British Library Cataloguing-in-Publication
Data. A catalogue record for this book is
available from the British Library.

ISSN 1355-4050
ISBN 0 948807 22 9

Printed and bound in Great Britain by
BPC Paulton Books Ltd.

CONTENTS

Introduction	1
Availability	2
Sizes and servings	3
Buying	3
Storing	4
Preparation	4
Grilling	5
Steaming	6
Poaching	7
Baking	7
Shallow frying	8
Deep frying	8
Stewing	8
Herbs to flavour cod	9
Spices to flavour cod	9
Marinades for cod	10
Sauces for cod	11
Glossary	12
Conversion tables	14
Chinese cod and tomato soup	16
Cod and prawn chowder	20
Cod grilled in a dish	24
Grilled cod cutlets Creole style	28
Cod with oranges and lemons	32

Cod kebabs	36
Cod with celery and walnut sauce	40
Cod and cockles in red wine	44
Deep fried cod with chips	47
Chinese smoked cod	51
Stir-fried cod with wheat and cucumber	55
Cod baked in a parcel	59
Cod in beer with peas	62
Cod patties with spiced tomato sauce	65
Special brown rice paella	69
Cod and prawn tart	72
Fisherman's pies	76
Smoked cod and potato bake	79
Smoked cod kedgeree	82
Smoked cod and french bean salad	86

INTRODUCTION

Cod is a fish with firm, white, chunky, flesh and a delicate flavour. It is an ocean fish that is never farmed and is readily available and extremely versatile. In some countries it is not caught during April and May, but it can always be bought frozen.

Cod is what is called a white fish. Its oil is concentrated in the liver making the flesh very low in fat, firm and white coloured. It is therefore high in protein and low in fat and calories, making it the perfect healthy food. It also contains significant amounts of B vitamins.

Cod is a round fish, as opposed to a flat fish such as plaice or sole. This means that they are slightly flattened from side to side with one eye on either side. Cod varies in size. The largest can weigh as much as 75 lb (34 kg) and the smallest, several pounds. The skin is greyish green on the back, mottled with olive, and shading to white under the belly.

Raw cod, filleted or sliced crossways into cutlets, freezes well and the flesh maintains its firmness during storage.

Cod can be grilled, poached, casseroled, fried

 1

or baked and its mild flavour blends with many different ingredients, making it a highly versatile protein food. Fry it with chips for a Friday night supper, grill or casserole it for an everyday meal, or turn it into soup or a gourmet dinner.

AVAILABILITY

Fresh cod should be available throughout the year, but it tends to become scarcer in April and May so it might be a little more expensive in those months.

Fresh cod can be bought from all fishmongers and supermarkets which have a fresh fish counter. It is usually sold either filleted or sliced crossways into cutlets, although small fish can be bought whole. These cutlets are also called cod steaks but, to avoid confusion with the frozen cod steaks (see below) the name cutlet has been used throughout the book.

Frozen cod fillets can be bought in packs of varying weight from most places that sell frozen food.

Cod steaks - small, rectangular blocks formed from pure cod, can be bought from the same source. Cooked plainly, these do not make a dish as attractive as one made from fillets or cutlets. They are, however, an extremely convenient food to keep in the freezer and are a useful and economical ingredient to use wherever flaked cod is required in a recipe. They can also be covered with thick sauces.

Yellow-coloured, smoked cod fillet is available fresh from fishmongers and fish counters in supermarkets. It can also be bought frozen. It is cold-smoked and therefore needs to be cooked.

SIZES AND SERVINGS

When you buy cod fillet there is no waste, apart from the skin.

However, it is very light and easy to eat and so a 6 oz (175 g) or 8 oz (225 g) portion per person has been used in the following recipes.

One cod cutlet is usually served per portion. Cutlets vary in size, according to the size of the original fish and whether the cutlets come from the head or the tail end. Generally, a cod cutlet weighs around 6 oz (175 g).

Allow 6 oz (175 g) smoked cod fillet per person. It has a rich, salty flavour and more than this amount would be too much.

If cod steaks are plainly cooked, serve two per person. Mixed in a dish with other ingredients, you may need to lower this amount.

BUYING

Cod is usually bought ready filleted or sliced into cutlets. When you are buying, make sure that the flesh is white and firm. A spongy texture or pink or grey colour shows poor quality. Fresh white fish should have little or no smell.

When buying, bear in mind the nature of your final dish. If a fillet is to be cut into four equal-sized portions, make sure that this is possible with the piece(s) of fish that you are offered. Will the thick end be more suitable than the thin? This is often a matter of personal taste but generally the thicker and middle parts are the best for serving in uncut portions and the thinner end is preferred for flaking or dicing.

When buying cutlets, your final dish will look better if you can choose them all of a similar size.

Never be afraid to ask a fishmonger for what you want. He will usually be pleased that someone is taking an interest in his fish and will willingly make sure that you buy what is best for your dish.

STORING

The sooner fish can be eaten after it is caught, the better it will taste. Ideally, cod should be eaten on the day of purchase. If not, it will keep in the refrigerator or a very cold larder for 24 hours. Store it in the wrapping in which you brought it home.

Cod freezes well. Cut fillets into equal-sized portions and place each one separately in a polythene bag. Put them all into a larger bag and seal the top. Store for up to one month. Pack and store cutlets in a similar way.

Thaw the fish in the refrigerator.

Frozen cod steaks can be kept for 1 - 2 months.

PREPARATION

Some dishes call for cod to be skinned before it is cooked. You will need a sharp knife and a clean, dry work surface.

To skin fillets, have the fillet with the narrower end pointing towards you, skin-side down. Work the blade of a sharp knife between the skin and the flesh on this narrow end and then hold on to the loosened skin keeping the skin firmly down on your work surface. Hold the knife blade downwards and pointing diagonally away from you. Gradually push it away from you and under the fish skin. You will find that the skin will come off easily.

If the fish has been frozen and is just beginning to thaw, you can simply loosen one end of the skin and pull it off by hand.

Cod cutlets also look best if they can be skinned. The process is the same as for fillets, although the cutlet is slightly more difficult to handle. Cutlets are horse-shoe shaped. Take one side of the horse shoe and work the knife between the skin and flesh. Turn the cutlet on its side and strip the skin away. You will find that it breaks off at the middle. Turn the cutlet over and skin the other side.

There will sometimes be a small piece of fin or bone sticking out of the skin at the centre of the cutlet. This can be cut away either parallel with the edge of the cutlet, or by cutting into the cutlet at either side of the bone. This is not essential but it makes a more pleasant-looking final dish which is easier to handle on the plate. The central bone of the cutlet is usually left in, although for some recipes it is pulled out after the first cooking stage.

After preparing any fish, it is a good idea to rub your hands and your work surface with a piece of cut lemon to eliminate fishy smells.

BASIC COOKING METHODS

Grilling. Cod can be grilled on a grill rack or in a dish. For grilling on a rack, fillets are usually left unskinned. Cutlets can be skinned if wished. Diced cod can also be made into kebabs for grilling.

As cod is a white fish, with no fats in its flesh,

it needs to be marinated in an oil mixture or well basted with oil or melted butter before grilling.

If your grill rack is one of the open kind, cover it with aluminium foil and pierce holes in the foil. To keep fillets moist as they cook, fill the bottom of the grill pan with hot water.

After marinating or basting the fish, heat the grill to high with the grill rack underneath the heat. Lay the fish on the hot rack. Cook the fillets for 5 - 7 minutes on one side only. Cook cutlets for about 5 minutes on each side. Check half way through cooking and baste the fish if necessary. If the fish is cooking too quickly, lower the heat to medium.

The fish is cooked when the flesh looks white and opaque and can be separated into moist flakes.

Fish grilled in a dish is often coated in a sauce or marinade. Both fillets and cutlets should be skinned and the fillets placed skin-side down. Fillets are not turned during cooking. Cutlets are turned once. Often, a sauce is poured in for the final stages of cooking.

Steaming. Steaming is the lightest method of all for cooking white fish. It is a method which is often used to make a dish for invalids but, as it brings out the true natural flavour of the fish, it can also be used as the first step in preparing more complicated dishes. Make sure that the cod is very fresh, and choose the thinnest end of the fillet.

Cut the fillet to size. Put the pieces onto a plate. Season them with salt and pepper and a little lemon juice. If you are using a steamer, lay the pieces of fish on buttered foil and bring the edges of the foil together to form a parcel, keeping the fish flat. If you are steaming over an ordinary saucepan, lay the fish on a metal plate and cover it with a second metal plate. Leave the fish for 30 minutes at room temperature.

To cook, if you are using a steamer, put water into the bottom and bring it to the boil. Lay the parcel of fish in the top part of the steamer and stand it over the water. Cover the steamer. If you are using a saucepan, bring water to the boil in the saucepan and place the fish between the two plates on top. In neither case must the water touch the fish container.

Steam the cod for about 15 minutes, or until it is cooked through.

To flavour steamed fish, a sprinkling of herbs or a dash of soy or Worcestershire sauce can be added just before cooking.

Poaching. Cod fillets and cutlets and also smoked cod fillets can be poached in a flavoured water or milk. The simplest way to do this is to put enough liquid (plain water, milk or a half-and-half mixture) to cover the fish into a shallow pan together with a bayleaf, a bouquet garni, a slice of onion, one teaspoon black peppercorns and a blade of mace. If you are using plain water you can also add a dash of white wine vinegar or a squeeze of lemon juice, or a slice of lemon.

Put in the fish and set the pan on a medium heat. Bring it to the boil and simmer the fish until it is cooked through. Thin fillets need 2 - 3 minutes cooking time, thicker cutlets about 8 minutes.

Baking. Heat the oven to 350F/180C/gas 4. Lay skinned cutlets or fillets in a buttered, oven proof dish. Season them and dot them with butter. Cover them with aluminium foil and put them into the oven for 30 minutes, or until they are cooked through.

Shallow Frying. This method is best for fillets. If the fish is simply fried, with an accompanying sauce, skinning is not necessary, but if it is fried first and finished off in a sauce, it is more pleasant to eat if skinned.

The fillets can be cut into single serving portions or into smaller pieces. Sprinkle them with salt, pepper and lemon juice and leave them at room temperature for 30 minutes. Coat them in seasoned flour.

Melt butter or heat oil in a large frying pan on a medium heat. Put in the pieces of fish, skinside up first, and cook them until they are golden brown on both sides.

The fish can be served quite plainly or a sauce can be made in the pan and the fish simmered in it for a few minutes before serving.

Deep Frying. Prepare cod fillets as for shallow frying. They may be deep fried with a flour coating or they may be dipped in batter after preparation.

Use a special deep fryer or a heavy saucepan and put into it enough vegetable oil to cover your piece of fish without filling the pan more than one third full.

Bring the oil to a temperature of 350F / 180C / gas 4. Flour or flour-and-batter the pieces of fish. Cook them, one at a time, until they are golden brown. This takes about 5 minutes. Lift out the pieces of fish and drain them on kitchen paper.

Stewing. Cod can be made into stews and soups with vegetables. Cut the cod into cubes. Fry the vegetables in hot oil or butter in a heat proof casserole or saucepan. Add the cooking liquid (fish or vegetable stock or a tomato juice) and bring it to the boil. Put in the cod and cook it in the boiling liquid for 1 minute so the heat seals in the juices. Turn the heat down and simmer the dish for a few more minutes or until the fish is just cooked through.

HERBS TO FLAVOUR COD

Cod has a light, delicate flavour, so add strongly-flavoured herbs sparingly.

Parsley, however, will not harm the flavour of cod and can be used quite liberally.

Other suitable herbs are fennel, chervil, basil and dill, which can be sprinkled on before cooking or which can be used to flavour sauces. Fennel, dill and chervil sprigs and whole basil leaves can be used as a garnish.

Marjoram and thyme are used in the more strongly flavoured dishes, and very sparingly in some marinades and sauces, but are not suitable for sprinkling over plainly-cooked cod.

SPICES TO FLAVOUR COD

The flavour of cod takes quite readily to spices which can be sprinkled sparingly onto the dry fish or mixed in slightly greater quantities into oil or melted butter for basting or for marinades. The best spices for cod are those with the more savoury flavours.

Cayenne or chili pepper is traditionally used for white fish instead of black or white pepper because of its cleaner flavour. Whichever cooking method you choose, use cayenne sparingly as it is very hot.

Paprika is often mixed with cayenne pepper

and can be used alone.

Curry spices go well with cod. Use cumin alone or mixed with coriander, turmeric and/or curry powder.

MARINADES FOR COD

4 tablespoons olive or sunflower oil and the juice of ½ lemon. The juice of 1 lime can be substituted for the lemon juice. Add to this mixture any of the following:

¼ teaspoon cayenne pepper and 1 teaspoon paprika;

¼ teaspoon cayenne pepper, 1 teaspoon paprika plus 1 tablespoon tomato purée;

1 teaspoon cumin;

½ teaspoon each cumin, coriander and turmeric;

½ teaspoon each cumin, coriander and turmeric plus 1 teaspoon curry powder;

1 tablespoon each chopped parsley and fennel;

2 tablespoons chopped chervil;

2 tablespoons chopped chervil or parsley plus 1 teaspoon mustard powder.

or 4 tablespoons olive oil and 1 tablespoon soy sauce. You may, if you wish, add to this mixture any of the following:

2 chopped spring onions;

1 teaspoon grated ginger root or 1 teaspoon bottled ginger purée;

1 teaspoon five-spice powder.

SAUCES FOR COD

Tomato Sauce
12 oz (350 g) tomatoes
1 oz (25 g) butter
1 tablespoon plain flour
½ pint (275 ml) vegetable stock (home-made, or from a good quality stock cube)
2 teaspoons tomato purée
bouquet garni

Quarter the tomatoes. Put the butter, flour and stock into a saucepan. Set them on a low to medium heat and bring them to the boil, stirring. Put in the tomatoes, tomato purée and bouquet garni. Simmer, uncovered, for 25 minutes. Strain the sauce through a sieve, pressing down hard with a wooden spoon to extract as much juice and tomato flesh as possible. Return the sauce to the rinsed pan and simmer it gently for 5 minutes so it becomes thick and smooth.

Parsley Sauce
½ pint (275 ml) fish or vegetable stock (home-made, or from a good quality stock cube)
1 oz (25 g) butter
2 tablespoons plain flour
6 tablespoons chopped parsley
1 tablespoon lemon juice
4 tablespoons double cream

Put the stock, butter and flour into a saucepan and set them on a medium heat. Stir until they come to the boil and you have a thick sauce. Stir in the parsley. Simmer on a low heat for 2 minutes. Stir in the lemon juice and cream.

GLOSSARY

Bouquet garni is a bunch of herbs which is used to flavour casseroles, pot roasts, poached meats, soups and stews. It usually contains parsley, thyme, marjoram and a bay leaf. Sometimes pieces of leek and/or celery are tied in with the herbs. Bouquets garni made from dried herbs tied in muslin, or in paper sachets like tea bags, are readily available.

Burghul wheat, also called bulgur or bulgar wheat, is made from whole wheat grains that have been soaked and then heated until they crack. It can be softened by soaking in cold water, or it can be cooked.

Cayenne pepper is a hot, red pepper with a sharp, clean flavour. It is produced by grinding several hot varieties of capsicum.

Chili powder is a mixture of cayenne pepper, paprika, cumin, cloves, marjoram and garlic, although the cayenne is the dominant flavour.

Chorizo Sausage is a speciality of Spain which can be bought at most delicatessens. It is hard-textured, red-coloured and spiced with paprika. It can be eaten raw, but is most often put into cooked dishes with a mixture of meats and/or vegetables.

Coriander is a herb. The leaves are used fresh and the seeds dried. The leaves are similar in appearance to flat parsley and their flavour and taste are spicy and pungent. The seeds have a sweet, spicy flavour and are often used in curries, either in ground form or coarsely crushed.

Cumin is a spice with a dry, pungent, slightly bitter flavour. It is frequently used in curries and is available ground or as whole seeds.

Five-spice powder is used in Chinese cookery. It is a mixture of anise pepper, star anise, cinnamon, cloves and fennel seed.

Lime pickle is hot and spicy, made from chopped whole limes. It is bitter, spicy and hot and should be used in cooked dishes in small quantities. It can also be served as a chutney with Indian dishes. Lime pickle is available from most supermarkets and delicatessens.

Mace is the outer covering of the nutmeg as it grows on the tree. Once dried it becomes bright yellow and it can be bought whole or ground. Whole mace is in the form of small, bright yellow chips. Ground mace is a bright ochre-coloured powder. The flavour of mace is similar to that of nutmeg but more delicate.

Muscovado sugar is unrefined brown sugar which is produced from sugar cane instead of from sugar beet. Both dark and light varieties are produced and any will be suitable for the recipes in this book. Ordinary sugar may be used if it is not available.

Paprika is a dark coloured, orange-red spice with a mild, aromatic, bitter-sweet flavour. It is produced by drying and grinding a mild species of capsicum.

Turmeric is a bright yellow spice with a mild, dry flavour. It is used in curries and also for colouring and flavouring rice both in India and the Middle East.

TABLE OF OVEN TEMPERATURES

	Fahrenheit (F)	Celsius (C)	Gas mark
	150	70	
	175	80	
	200	100	
Very cool	225	110	¼
	250	120	½
	275	140	1
Cool	300	150	2
Warm	325	160	3
Moderate/ Medium	350	180	4
Fairly Hot	375	190	5
	400	200	6
Hot	425	220	7
	450	230	8
Very hot	475	240	9
	500	260	9

IMPERIAL/METRIC CONVERSIONS

Dry weight		Liquid measure	
ounces	grams	fluid ounces	millilitres
1	25	1	25
2	50	2	50
3	75	3	75-90
4 (¼ lb)	125	4	125
5	150	5 (¼ pint)	150
6	175	6	175
7	200	7	200
8 (½ lb)	225	8	225
9	250	9	250
10	275	10 (½ pint)	275
11	300	11	300
12 (¾ lb)	350	12	350
13	375	13	375
14	400	14	400
15	425	15 (¾ pint)	425
16 (1 lb)	450	16	450
17	475	17	475
18	500	18	500
2¼ lb	1000 (1 kilo)	20 (1 pint)	550
		1¾ pints	1000 (1 litre)

CHINESE COD AND TOMATO SOUP

Serves: 4
Type of dish: hot first course
Suitable for main course: no
Preparation start time: 40 minutes before serving
Preparation time: 30 minutes
Waiting time: nil
Cooking time: 5 minutes
Suitable for dinner parties: yes
Special equipment: saucepan
Suitable for microwave cooking: no
Suitable for pressure cooking: no
Suitable for freezing: yes
Calorie content: low
Carbohydrate content: low
Fibre content: low
Protein content: high
Fat content: low

1 lb (450 g) cod fillet
1 teaspoon salt
1 tablespoon cornflour
2 tablespoons rice wine or dry sherry
12 oz (350 g) tomatoes
4 spring onions
½ oz (15 g) fresh ginger root, or 1 teaspoon ginger purée
1½ pints fish or chicken stock (see below)
2 tablespoons soy sauce
3 tablespoons chopped fresh coriander

Skin the cod and cut it into 1 inch (2.5 cm) squares. In a bowl, mix it with the salt, cornflour and rice wine or sherry.

Put the tomatoes into a bowl and cover them with boiling water. Leave them for 2 minutes and peel away the skins. Chop the tomatoes. Finely chop the spring onions. Peel and finely grate the ginger root.

Put the stock into a saucepan and bring it to the boil. Put in the fish, tomatoes, spring onions, ginger root and soy sauce. Simmer, uncovered, for 5 minutes.

Stir in the coriander just before serving.

☆   ☆   ☆

Chef's tips:
☆ Chinese soup is traditionally served in china bowls and eaten with china spoons.
☆ In an authentic Chinese meal, there would be no accompaniment to this soup. However, warm, crisp white rolls go well.

☆ Parsley can be used instead of coriander.
☆ Do not use a highly-flavoured stock cube for this soup. Either buy good quality cubes that have a mild, natural flavour, or make the stock yourself. To make fish stock, use the skin from the cod. Put it into a saucepan with an onion, a carrot and a stick of celery, all roughly chopped, plus 1 teaspoon black peppercorns, a pinch of salt and a pinch of mixed herbs. Add 2 pints (1.15 litres) water and bring everything to the boil. Simmer for 30 minutes, uncovered, and then strain the stock. Either use it immedi-

ately or keep it, covered, in the refrigerator for up to three days. It can also be frozen for up to one month.

☆ To freeze the soup, do not add the coriander. Cool the soup completely. Put it into a rigid container and cover it. Store it for up to one month. Thaw in the refrigerator and reheat gently.

COD AND PRAWN CHOWDER

Serves: 4
Type of dish: hot main course
Suitable for first course: yes, see below
Preparation start time: 2 hours 15 minutes before serving
1st preparation time: 30 minutes
1st cooking time: 30 minutes
Waiting time: nil
2nd cooking time: 35 minutes
2nd preparation time: 30 minutes
Suitable for dinner parties: yes, as first course
Special equipment: saucepan; liquidiser
Suitable for microwave cooking: yes
Suitable for pressure cooking: yes
Suitable for freezing: yes
Calorie content: medium
Carbohydrate content: medium
Fibre content: medium
Protein content: high
Fat content: medium

1 lb (450 g) cod fillet

fish stock:
1 carrot
1 celery stick
1 small onion
1 teaspoon black peppercorns
bouquet garni or ½ teaspoon dried mixed herbs

soup:
1 head celery
1½ lb (675 g) potatoes
1 large onion
1½ oz (40 g) butter
1 pint (550 ml) milk
½ teaspoon salt
¼ teaspoon cayenne pepper
6 oz (175 g) peeled prawns
one 12 oz (350 g) can sweetcorn
4 tablespoons chopped parsley

For the *fish stock,* roughly chop the carrot, celery and onion. Put them into a saucepan with the skin from the fish, the peppercorns, bouquet garni and 3 pints (1.65 litres) cold water. Bring them to the boil and simmer, uncovered, for 30 minutes. Strain and reserve the liquid.

For the *soup,* cut the cod into pieces about ½ inch (1.3 cm) square. Finely chop the celery. Peel and finely chop the potatoes and onion. Melt the butter in a saucepan on a low heat. Put in the celery, potatoes and onion. Cover them and cook them gently for 10 minutes. Pour in the milk and 2 pints (1.15 litres) of the reserved stock. Add the salt and the cayenne pepper. Cover and simmer for 30 minutes. Put in the cod and simmer for 5 minutes more so it is cooked through.

Liquidise half the soup. Return it to the rest and reheat gently. Add the prawns, corn and parsley and simmer for 5 minutes, or until they are just heated through.

Chef's tips·

☆ As a main course, serve in large, deep bowls and accompany the soup with fresh, crusty bread or rolls and a green salad.

☆ The soup makes an ideal first course to serve before a light meal such as a salad. Use smaller bowls. Bread may be served with it if wished.

☆ To freeze, do not add the prawns, sweetcorn and parsley. Cool the soup completely. Put it into a rigid container and cover it. Store it for up to one month. Thaw in the refrigerator, re-heat and add the prawns, corn and parsley as above.

COD GRILLED IN A DISH

Serves: 4
Type of dish: hot main course (two recipes)
Suitable for first course: yes, see below
Preparation start time: 1 hour before serving
Preparation time: 40 minutes
Waiting time: nil
Cooking time: 15 minutes
Suitable for dinner parties: yes
Special equipment: grill and heatproof dish
Suitable for microwave cooking: yes
Suitable for pressure cooking: no
Suitable for freezing: no
Calorie content: medium
Carbohydrate content: low
Fibre content: low
Protein content: high
Fat content: medium

4 cod cutlets, each about 1 inch (2.5 cm) thick, or 2 lb (900 g) cod fillet
for Cod with Curry and Orange:
1½ oz (40 g) butter
2 teaspoons curry powder
1 teaspoon ground turmeric
grated rind and juice ½ medium orange
1 garlic clove, crushed with pinch salt
for Cod with Lemon and Parsley:
1½ oz (40 g) butter
4 tablespoons chopped parsley
grated rind and juice 1 lemon
pinch salt
freshly-ground black pepper

Skin the cod cutlets and remove the small bones in the top (page 5). Skin the fillets (page 4). Put the cutlets or fillets all together in a large, shallow, heatproof dish.

For *Cod with Curry and Orange*, put the butter, curry powder, turmeric, orange rind and juice and garlic into a saucepan and set them on a low heat. Leave them until the butter has melted. Pour the curry mixture over the cod, turning the pieces of fish to make sure that they are well coated on both sides.

For the *Cod with Lemon and Parsley*, put the butter, parsley and lemon rind into a saucepan and season them. Set them on a low heat and leave them until the butter has melted. Pour the butter mixture over the cod and turn the pieces of fish so they become well coated on both sides.

In both cases, leave the cod fillets skin side

 25

down.

Heat the grill to high. Put the dish under the heat. Cook the cutlets for about 6 minutes on each side, and the fillets for about 7 minutes altogether.

Chef's tips

☆ Serve straight from the dish. The *Cod with*

Curry and Orange can be garnished with parsley sprigs or small orange twists. The *Cod with Lemon and Parsley* can be garnished with lemon twists or wedges.

☆ Serve with a selection of lightly cooked vegetables, and sauté, croquette or plainly-boiled potatoes.

☆ To serve as a first course, reduce the cod fillet to about 3 oz (75 g) per person, but use the same quantity of other ingredients.

GRILLED COD CUTLETS CREOLE STYLE

Serves: 4
Type of dish: hot main course
Suitable for first course: no
Preparation start time: 2 hours before serving
Preparation time: 45 minutes (overlaps waiting time)
Waiting time: 50 minutes
Cooking time: 15 minutes
Suitable for dinner parties: yes
Special equipment: grill, grill pan
Suitable for microwave cooking: yes
Suitable for pressure cooking: yes
Suitable for freezing: no
Calorie content: medium
Carbohydrate content: low
Fibre content: low
Protein content: high
Fat content: low

4 cod cutlets, each about 1 inch (2.5 cm) thick
1 lb (450 g) ripe tomatoes
1 green pepper
1 celery stick
1 onion
1 garlic clove
3 tablespoons olive or sunflower oil
¼ teaspoon chili powder
1 teaspoon paprika
2 tablespoons white wine vinegar
1 teaspoon Muscovado sugar

Put the tomatoes into a bowl. Pour boiling water over them and leave them for 2 minutes. Drain, skin and finely chop them. Finely chop the pepper, celery stick, onion and garlic. Heat the oil in a saucepan on a low heat. Put in the chopped vegetables and garlic and cook them gently for about 5 minutes, or until they are soft and just beginning to brown. Stir in the chili powder and paprika, tomatoes, vinegar and sugar. Cover and cook gently for 20 minutes, or until you have a thick sauce. Turn the sauce into a shallow dish and let it cool completely.

Skin the cod cutlets and remove as many of the bones as possible (page 5). Turn the cutlets in the cooled sauce and leave them for 30 minutes at room temperature. Take the cutlets out of the sauce. Put the sauce once again into a saucepan and reheat it gently.

Preheat the grill to high and, if you have an open, wire rack, cover it with foil. Lay the cutlets on the hot rack and cook them for about 6 minutes on each side or until they are quite cooked through.

Put a portion of the sauce onto each of four dinner plates and put a cod cutlet on top.

☆   ☆   ☆

Chef's tips:
☆ Garnish the fish with parsley sprigs or with thin strips of green pepper.
☆ Serve with rice, either plain or flavoured with paprika, chili powder and tomato purée.
☆ A green salad, sweetcorn kernels or baby sweetcorn, or lightly-cooked green vegetables

make the best accompaniments.

☆ This recipe can also be made with cod fillet. Use four pieces of cod fillet, each weighing around 8 oz (225 g). Do not skin them. To cook, pour a little hot water into the bottom of the grill pan. If you are covering the grill rack with foil, pierce holes in the foil to allow the steam through. Lay the fillets on the hot grill rack, skin side down, and cook them on one side only for 7 - 8 minutes, or until they are cooked through.

COD WITH ORANGES AND LEMONS

Serves: 4
Type of dish: hot main course
Suitable for first course: no
Preparation start time: 3½ hours before serving
1st preparation time: 20 minutes
Waiting time: 2 hours
2nd preparation time: 20 minutes
Cooking time: 30 minutes (including making sauce)
Suitable for dinner parties: yes
Special equipment: grill; grill rack
Suitable for microwave cooking: no
Suitable for pressure cooking: no
Suitable for freezing: no
Calorie content: medium
Carbohydrate content: low
Fibre content: low
Protein content: high
Fat content: medium

2 lb (900 g) cod fillet
2 small onions
1 garlic clove
2 tablespoons olive or sunflower oil
3 medium oranges
1 lemon
salt
freshly-ground black pepper
3 celery sticks
1 small carrot
1 teaspoon black peppercorns
bouquet garni
1 oz (25 g) butter
2 tablespoons plain flour
1 tablespoon grated Parmesan cheese

Skin the cod (page 4) and reserve the skin. Cut the cod into four even-sized pieces.

Thinly slice one of the onions. Finely chop the garlic clove. Put them into a large, shallow dish. Put in the oil. Grate in the rind from one quarter of one of the oranges and one quarter of the lemon. Squeeze the juice from half the lemon and half the orange and add 1 tablespoon each to the marinade. Season the marinade lightly. Turn the pieces of cod in the marinade and leave them at room temperature for 2 hours, turning them several times.

To make the stock, roughly chop the remaining onion, one celery stick and the carrot. Put them into a saucepan with the fish skin, the peppercorns and bouquet garni. Pour in 1½ pints

(825 ml) water. Bring them to the boil, cover and simmer for 1 hour. Strain and reserve the liquid.

Finely chop the remaining celery sticks. Melt the butter in a saucepan on a low heat. Put in the celery, cover it and cook it gently for 10 minutes. Stir in the flour plus ¾ pint (425 ml) of the fish stock. Bring them to the boil, stirring, and simmer, uncovered, for 5 minutes. Grate in the rinds of ¼ lemon and ¼ orange and add 1 tablespoon each of the orange and lemon juices. Set this sauce aside.

Having cut the rind and pith (and discarded them) from the remaining two oranges, thinly slice the flesh.

Lift the fish out of the marinade, leaving a few pieces of onion still clinging to it. Lay it in a shallow, heatproof serving dish, skin side down.

Heat the grill to the highest temperature. Put the fish under the grill and cook it, without turning, for 7 minutes, or until it is cooked through. Pour the sauce over the fish. Lay a slice of orange on each piece of fish and sprinkle a little of the Parmesan cheese over the top. Return the dish to the grill to brown the cheese. Serve straight from the dish.

☆   ☆   ☆

Chef's tips:

☆ Parsley, chervil or coriander sprigs may be used for garnish if wished.

☆ Serve with a green salad or a selection of lightly-cooked green vegetables; plus jacket potatoes, sauté potatoes or plainly-boiled new potatoes tossed with butter and parsley.

☆ A good quality fish or vegetable stock cube may be used instead of making the stock.

COD KEBABS

Serves: 4
Type of dish: hot main course
Suitable for first course: yes, see below
Preparation start time: 1½ hours before serving
1st preparation time: 20 minutes
Waiting time: 30 minutes
2nd preparation time: 30 minutes
Cooking time: 10 minutes
Suitable for dinner parties: yes
Special equipment: kebab skewers; grill
Suitable for microwave cooking: no
Suitable for pressure cooking: no
Suitable for freezing: no
Calorie content: medium
Carbohydrate content: low
Fibre content: low
Protein content: high
Fat content: medium

1½ lb (675 g) cod fillet
for Cod Kebabs with Lemon:
juice 2 lemons
3 fl oz (90 ml) olive oil
2 teaspoons ground cumin
4 bay leaves
freshly-ground black pepper
4 small onions
1 green pepper
for Cod Kebabs with Lime:
juice 2 limes
3 fl oz (90 ml) olive oil
2 teaspoons paprika
¼ teaspoon cayenne pepper
4 small tomatoes
1 red pepper
garnish:
8 oz (225 g) tomatoes
2 oz (50 g) parsley, chopped
1 lemon, cut into wedges; or 1 lime, cut into wedges, depending on recipe used

Skin the fish (page 4) and cut it into 1 inch cubes.

For the *Kebabs with Lemon:* in a bowl, mix together the lemon juice, oil, cumin, bay leaves and pepper. Turn the fish in the mixture and leave it for 30 minutes at room temperature.

Peel the onions. Bring a saucepan of water to the boil. Put in the onions and simmer them for 5 minutes. Drain them. Pour boiling water over the green pepper. Leave it for 5 minutes and drain it. Core and seed it and cut it into 1 inch (2.5 cm) squares.

Thread the fish cubes, green pepper and pieces of bay leaf onto four kebab skewers. Roll the onions in the marinade and use them to top each skewer.

For the *Kebabs with Lime:* in a bowl mix together the lime juice, oil, paprika and cayenne pepper. Turn the fish in the mixture and leave it for 30 minutes at room temperature. Pour boiling water over the pepper, leave it for 5 minutes and drain it. Cut it into 1 inch (2.5 cm) squares. Pour boiling water over the tomatoes. Leave them for 2 minutes, drain and skin them.

Thread the fish cubes and pieces of pepper onto four kebab skewers. Top each skewer with a skinned tomato.

To cook, heat the grill to high and, if you have an open wire rack, cover it with foil. Lay the kebabs on the hot rack and cook them for 6 - 7 minutes, turning them several times, until the cod is cooked through.

Serve either type of kebab on a bed of chopped parsley and garnished with the tomato and lemon wedges.

Chef's tips:
☆ Serve with a savoury rice and a green or mixed salad.
☆ For a first course, halve the amount of fish and keep the rest of the ingredients the same. Use small skewers.

COD WITH CELERY AND WALNUT SAUCE

Serves: 4
Type of dish: hot main course
Suitable for first course: no
Preparation start time: 2 hours before serving
1st preparation time: 20 minutes
1st cooking time: 1 hour (stock)
Waiting time: 1 hour, concurrent with first cook-
  ing time
2nd cooking time: 30 minutes
Suitable for dinner parties: yes
Special equipment: large, heavy frying pan
Suitable for microwave cooking: no
Suitable for pressure cooking: no
Suitable for freezing: no
Calorie content: medium
Carbohydrate content: low
Fibre content: low
Protein content: high
Fat content: medium

2 lb (900 g) cod fillet

stock:
1 small carrot
1 small celery stick
handful celery leaves
1 small onion
1 teaspoon black peppercorns
bouquet garni

finished dish:
juice 1 lemon
1½ oz (40 g) plain flour
salt
freshly-ground black pepper
4 tablespoons olive or sunflower oil
4 large celery sticks
2 oz (50 g) shelled walnuts or walnut pieces
1 small onion
1 garlic clove
4 tablespoons white wine vinegar

Skin the cod (page 4). Cut it into even-sized serving pieces. Put them into a flat dish and sprinkle them with lemon juice. Leave them at room temperature for 1 hour.

For the stock, roughly chop the carrot, celery and onion. Put them into a saucepan with the fish skin, celery leaves, peppercorns and bouquet garni. Add 1¼ pints (725 ml) water. Bring them to the boil, cover and simmer for 1 hour. Strain and reserve the liquid.

Put the flour onto a plate and season it well. Use the flour to coat the pieces of fish and reserve any remainder. Finely chop the celery, walnuts, onion and garlic.

Heat 2 tablespoons of the oil in a large, heavy frying pan on a medium heat. Put in the pieces of fish and fry them, skin side down first, until they are golden. Transfer them to a serving dish and keep them warm. If necessary, do this in several batches, adding more oil when needed.

Put the celery, walnuts, onion and garlic into the pan and cook them until the onion is soft, stirring frequently. Stir in 3 tablespoons of the remaining flour and ¾ pint (425 ml) of the stock. Bring the sauce to the boil, stirring. Add the vinegar and simmer for 2 minutes. Pour the sauce over the fish to serve.

☆　　☆　　☆

Chef's tips:

☆ Garnish with celery leaves, parsley sprigs or chopped parsley and/or walnut halves.

☆ Serve with a colourful, contrasting vegetable such as spinach, carrots or broccoli; plus sauté potatoes, potato croquettes, creamed potatoes or plainly-boiled new potatoes tossed with butter and parsley.

☆ A good quality fish stock cube may be used instead of making the stock.

COD AND COCKLES IN RED WINE

Serves: 4
Type of dish: hot main course
Suitable for first course: no
Preparation start time: 1 hour before serving
Preparation time: 30 minutes
Waiting time: nil
Cooking time: 30 minutes
Suitable for dinner parties: yes
Special equipment: large, heavy frying pan with lid
Suitable for microwave cooking: no
Suitable for pressure cooking: no
Suitable for freezing: no
Calorie content: high
Carbohydrate content: low
Fibre content: low
Protein content: high
Fat content: medium

1½ lb (675 g) cod fillet
8 oz (225 g) cockles
2 tablespoons flour
pepper
4 rashers lean back bacon, thin cut
1 large onion
6 oz (175 g) button mushrooms
1½ oz (40 g) butter
7 fl oz (200ml) dry red wine
2 tablespoons chopped parsley
1 tablespoon chopped thyme (or ½ teaspoon dried)

Skin the cod fillet (page 4) and cut it into 1 inch (2.5 cm) cubes. Season the flour with the pepper. Coat the pieces of fish in the seasoned flour. Chop the bacon. Thinly slice the onion and quarter the mushrooms.

Melt half the butter in a large frying pan on a low heat. Put in the bacon and onion and cook them until the onions are golden, about 15 minutes. Remove them. Raise the heat very slightly and put in the cubes of cod. Brown them on all sides for about 3 minutes or until they are cooked through but still firm. Remove them.

Add the rest of the butter to the pan and raise the heat to medium. Put in the cockles and mushrooms and stir them on the heat for 2 minutes. Pour in the wine and stir until it boils. Lower the heat to simmer and stir in the herbs. Carefully replace the fish and the onion and bacon. Turn the fish over in the sauce, taking care not to break it up. Simmer gently for 3 minutes.

To serve, lay the fish on a warmed serving dish and spoon the sauce over the top.

Chef's tips:
☆ Garnish with chopped parsley. Thin triangles of toast, made from white bread and with the crusts removed, can also look very attractive.
☆ Serve with plainly boiled potatoes, sauté potatoes or croquette potatoes.
☆ A green salad is the best vegetable accompaniment.

DEEP FRIED COD WITH CHIPS

Serves: 4
Type of dish: hot main course
Suitable for first course: no
Preparation start time: 2 hours before serving
Preparation time: 45 minutes
Waiting time: 50 minutes
Cooking time: 30 minutes
Suitable for dinner parties: no
Special equipment: pan suitable for deep frying, with basket; deep fat thermometer
Suitable for microwave cooking: no
Suitable for pressure cooking: no
Suitable for freezing: no
Calorie content: high
Carbohydrate content: medium
Fibre content: low
Protein content: high
Fat content: medium

4 cod fillets, each about 6 oz (175 g)
2 oz (50 g) plain flour, seasoned
1½ lb (675 g) potatoes
2 - 3 pints (1.2 - 1.75 litres) sunflower or corn oil, for deep frying
batter:
4 oz (125 g) plain flour
pinch salt
2 tablespoons sunflower or corn oil
¼ pint (150 ml) cold water
1 large egg white

Peel the potatoes and cut them into chips about ½ inch (1.2 cm) thick. Soak them in a bowl of water for 30 minutes. Drain them and wrap them in a tea cloth. Leave them to dry for 20 minutes.

Heat the oven to 300F/150C/gas 2.

To make the batter, put the flour into a bowl with the salt. Make a well in the centre and pour in the oil and water. Gradually beat in flour from the sides of the well until you have a thick, creamy batter. Put the batter into the refrigerator for 15 minutes to chill.

Coat the cod fillets in the seasoned flour.

Gently heat the deep oil, putting a deep fat thermometer into the pan.

When the oil has reached a temperature of 350F/180C/gas 4, put in about one quarter of the chips. Remove them as soon as the bubbling in the pan subsides. Reheat the oil, if necessary, before putting in the next batch. When all the chips have been removed, heat the oil to 400F/200C/gas 6. Put the chips back into the hot oil,

again in several batches, and cook them until they are crisp and golden brown. Put them into a dish that is lined with crumpled kitchen paper and put them into the oven to keep warm.

While the chips are frying, whisk the egg white until it is stiff and fold it into the batter. Put the batter into a deep bowl and place the bowl near the cooker.

When the chips are in the oven, let the oil cool to 350F/180C/gas 4. Dip a piece of fish into the batter. Lift it out with a skewer or a fork and let it drain for a few seconds over the bowl. Lower it into the oil and fry it until the batter is crisp and golden and the fish is cooked through (3 to 5 minutes, depending on the thickness of the fish). Lift the fish out with a skewer and place it on crumpled kitchen paper to drain. Cook the other pieces in the same way.

☆   ☆   ☆

Chef's tips:
☆ Traditionally, fish and chips are served without vegetable accompaniments.
☆ Lighten the flavour by serving tartare sauce, tomato sauce or simply wedges of lemon alongside the fish.
☆ The cod fillets may be skinned if wished.
☆ Preparation and waiting times overlap slightly.
☆ If you do not have a deep fat thermometer, you can test the temperature of the oil by dropping in one chip. At 350F/180C/gas 4, it should sink to the bottom of the pan and gently bubble.

CHINESE SMOKED COD

Serves: 4
Type of dish: hot or cold main course
Suitable for first course: yes, see below
1st preparation time: 20 minutes
1st waiting time: 1 hour
Cooking time: 30 minutes
2nd preparation time: 20 minutes
2nd waiting time: 1 hour, for cooling
Preparation start time: 3 hours 15 minutes before serving
Suitable for dinner parties: yes
Special equipment: pan suitable for deep frying
Suitable for microwave cooking: no
Suitable for pressure cooking: no
Suitable for freezing: no
Calorie content: medium
Carbohydrate content: low
Fibre content: low
Protein content: high
Fat content: medium

1½ lb (675 g) cod fillet
½ oz (15 g) fresh ginger root, or 1 teaspoon ginger purée
4 spring onions
1 garlic clove
4 tablespoons rice wine or dry sherry
2 tablespoons soy sauce
½ teaspoon five-spice powder
2 tablespoons Muscovado sugar
oil for deep frying
1 tablespoon cornflour
¼ pint (150 ml) stock or water

Skin the fish and cut it into 1 inch (2.5 cm) cubes. Peel and grate the ginger root. Finely chop two of the spring onions and the garlic. Mix together the ginger, onions, garlic, rice wine or sherry, soy sauce, five-spice powder and sugar. Turn the fish in the marinade and leave it for 1 hour at room temperature. Lift out the fish and reserve the marinade.

Heat a pan of deep oil to 350F/180C/gas 4. Put in the pieces of fish, a few at a time, and deep fry them until they are golden brown. Lift them out and drain them on kitchen paper. Fry the rest of the pieces in the same way.

Put the cornflour into a bowl and stir in 4 tablespoons of the stock or water. Put the remaining stock or water into a saucepan with the marinade on a medium heat. Stir in the cornflour mixture and stir on the heat until the sauce boils and thickens. Take the pan from the heat and pour the sauce into a dish. Put the pieces of cod into the sauce and leave them until they and the sauce are quite cold.

Cut the remaining spring onions into 3 inch (7.5 cm) lengths. Make four one-inch (2.5 cm deep) cuts in each end of the onion pieces. Put the pieces into a bowl of ice-cold water and leave them until the ends curl outwards.

Serve the cod either cold, or reheated gently in the sauce when needed.

Chef's tips:

☆ Serve garnished with the spring onion brushes.

☆ Small amounts of the cod can be served as a first course in small bowls.

☆ In an authentic Chinese meal, this fish dish would be a course on its own, served in small bowls with no accompaniment. To serve it as a main meal, have plainly-cooked rice and either a salad or stir-fried vegetables as an accompaniment.

☆ The 'smoked' in the title may be misleading. The fish is not smoked either before the cooking process or during it, but the marinade and the method used give it a smoked flavour.

☆ Five-spice powder: see glossary (page 12).

STIR-FRIED COD WITH WHEAT AND CUCUMBER

Serves: 4
Type of dish: hot main course
Suitable for first course: no
Preparation start time: 1½ hours before serving
1st preparation time: 15 minutes
Waiting time: 30 minutes
2nd preparation time: 15 minutes
Cooking time: 30 minutes
Suitable for dinner parties: no
Special equipment: saucepan; large, heavy frying pan
Suitable for microwave cooking: no
Suitable for pressure cooking: no
Suitable for freezing: no
Calorie content: medium
Carbohydrate content: high
Fibre content: high
Protein content: high
Fat content: medium

1½ lb (675 g) cod fillet
juice 1 lemon
1 teaspoon salt
freshly-ground black pepper
1 medium onion
1 garlic clove
one 14 oz (400 g) can chopped tomatoes in juice
water to make up 1 pint (550ml) liquid
1 large cucumber
4 tablespoons olive or sunflower oil
8 oz (225 g) burghul wheat
up to 2 oz (50 g) butter
2 boxes salad cress

Skin the cod and cut it into ¾ inch (2 cm) pieces. Put it into a dish. Sprinkle it with half the lemon juice, half the salt and some pepper. Leave it at room temperature for 30 minutes.

Finely chop the onion and garlic. Measure the liquid volume of the tomatoes and juice together and make it up to 1 pint (575 ml) with water. Cut the cucumber into 1 inch (2.5 ml) sticks.

Heat the oil in a saucepan on a low heat. Put in the onion and garlic and soften them. Put in the wheat and cook it for 1 minute, stirring. Pour in the tomatoes and water. Bring them to the boil. Put in the remaining salt, cover and simmer for 20 minutes, or until the wheat is tender and all the liquid has been absorbed. Keep the wheat warm.

Melt the butter in a large frying pan on a high heat. Put in half the cucumber and stir-fry it for

2 minutes. Add it to the wheat. Put in the remaining cucumber and cook it in the same way. Add it to the wheat. Add extra butter to the pan if necessary. Put in half the cod and stir-fry it for about 2 minutes, or until it is cooked through but still firm. Add it to the wheat and treat the remaining fish in the same way. Very carefully, so as not to break up the fish, fold one box of the salad cress into the wheat.

Transfer the wheat and fish to a serving dish and garnish with the remaining cress.

Chef's tips:

☆ For a light meal, you may find that the dish needs no other accompaniment. Certainly no potatoes or bread are necessary. A mixture of stir-fried vegetables goes well.

☆ Burghul wheat: see glossary (page 12).

☆ Stir-frying means moving small pieces of food in oil or butter on a high heat so they just cook through. Stir-fried fish should stay firm and not break up. The Chinese use a wok for stir-frying, but a large, heavy frying pan will work just as well.

Cod Baked in a Parcel

COD BAKED IN A PARCEL

Serves: 4
Type of dish: hot main course
Suitable for first course: yes, see below
Preparation start time: 1 hour before serving
Preparation time: 30 minutes
Waiting time: nil
Cooking time: 20 minutes
Suitable for dinner parties: yes
Special equipment: oven, oven tray, foil
Suitable for microwave cooking: no
Suitable for pressure cooking: no
Suitable for freezing: no
Calorie content: medium
Carbohydrate content: low
Fibre content: low
Protein content: high
Fat content: low

for Cod with Cheese:
1½ lb (675 g) cod fillet
juice ½ lemon
1 tablespoon Worcestershire sauce
4 tablespoons chopped parsley
butter for greasing
3 oz (75 g) Cheddar cheese, grated
for Cod with Tomatoes:
2 lb (900 g) cod fillet
salt
freshly-ground black pepper
12 oz (350 g) tomatoes
2 tablespoons chopped basil, or 1 teaspoon dried
butter for greasing

For each recipe, skin the cod fillet and cut it into ½ inch (1.3 cm) cubes. Put it into a bowl. Heat the oven to 350F/180C/gas 4.

For the *Cod with Cheese,* mix together the lemon juice and Worcestershire sauce. Pour them over the cod. Add the parsley and gently fold the ingredients together.

For the *Cod with Tomatoes,* season the cod.

Put the tomatoes into a bowl. Pour boiling water over them and leave them for two minutes. Drain, skin and finely chop them. Put them with the cod and add the basil. Gently mix the ingredients together.

For both recipes, cut four pieces of foil about 10 inches (25 cm) square and butter them. Divide the cod and other ingredients between them. For the *Cod with Cheese,* scatter the cheese over the top at this point. Bring two sides of the foil together and seal them along the top. Fold the ends of the packets upwards and over several times to seal them. Lay the foil packets on a baking sheet.

Put the packets into the oven for 20 minutes. To serve, unwrap the packets onto warmed, individual plates.

Chef's tips:

☆ Serve with a selection of lightly cooked vegetables such as peas, mange tout peas, broccoli, cauliflower or green or broad beans; and sauté potatoes or plainly boiled new potatoes tossed with butter and parsley.

☆ If basil is not available use chervil or parsley.

☆ One diced, green pepper may be added to the *Cod with Tomatoes,* if wished.

☆ Baking parchment can be used instead of foil.

☆ To serve as a first course. *Cod with Cheese:* use 12 oz (350 g) cod, 1 tablespoon lemon juice, 2 teaspoons Worcestershire sauce, 2 tablespoons parsley and 2 oz (50 g) cheese. Bake in one large parcel. *Cod with Tomatoes:* use 12 oz (350 g) cod, 6 oz (175 g) tomatoes and 1 tablespoon basil. Bake in one large parcel. Serve both in small ramekin dishes.

COD IN BEER WITH PEAS

Serves: 4
Type of dish: hot main course
Suitable for first course: yes, see below
Preparation start time: 1½ hours before serving
1st preparation time: 30 minutes
Waiting time: nil
Cooking time: 20 minutes
2nd preparation time: 30 minutes
Suitable for dinner parties: yes
Special equipment: oven; large, shallow, oven-
    proof dish; greaseproof paper
Suitable for microwave cooking: yes
Suitable for pressure cooking: no
Suitable for freezing: no
Calorie content: medium
Carbohydrate content: medium
Fibre content: medium
Protein content: high
Fat content: medium

4 cod cutlets
butter for greasing
¼ nutmeg, freshly grated, or ¼ teaspoon ground nutmeg
I medium onion
I bayleaf
½ pint (275 ml) bitter beer
12 oz (350 g) shelled peas, fresh or frozen
I oz (25 g) butter
I heaped tablespoon plain flour
2 teaspoons malt vinegar
4 tablespoons chopped parsley

Heat the oven to 350F/180C/gas 4. Lightly butter a large, shallow, ovenproof dish. Put in the cod cutlets and grate or sprinkle the nutmeg over them. Thinly slice the onion and scatter it over the top. Put in the bayleaf. Pour in the beer. Cover the fish with buttered greaseproof paper. Put the dish into the oven for 30 minutes, or until the fish is cooked through.

Lift out the cutlets. Skin them and remove any bones. Lay them on a warmed serving dish and keep them warm. Strain and reserve the cooking liquids.

Melt the butter in a saucepan on a low heat. Put in the peas, cover, and gently simmer them for 5 minutes. Stir in the flour and then the cooking liquids. Stir until the liquid boils and thickens. Simmer for 2 minutes. Stir in the vinegar and chopped parsley.

Pour the peas and sauce over the fish.

Chef's tips:

☆ Garnish with sprigs of parsley or chervil

☆ Serve with plainly-boiled new potatoes tossed with butter and parsley, with sauté potatoes, creamed potatoes or potato croquettes.

☆ Serve one other contrasting vegetable, such as carrots or broccoli.

☆ To serve as a first course, use 12 oz (350 g) cod fillet, not cutlets. Skin it before cooking in the same way, using just a sprinkling of nutmeg, one small onion and ¼ pint (150 ml) beer. Dice the fish and put it into small dishes. Use 6 oz (175 g) peas, 1 oz (25 g) butter, ½ tablespoon flour for the sauce. Pour the finished sauce over the fish and garnish with parsley sprigs.

COD PATTIES WITH SPICED TOMATO SAUCE

Serves: 4
Type of dish: hot main course
Suitable for first course: yes, see below
Preparation start time: 2 hours before serving
1st preparation time: 15 minutes
Waiting time: nil
1st cooking time: 20 minutes
2nd preparation time: 1 hour
2nd cooking time: 15 minutes
Suitable for dinner parties: yes
Special equipment: oven; frying pan
Suitable for microwave cooking: fish can be initially cooked in microwave
Suitable for pressure cooking: no
Suitable for freezing: no
Caloric content: medium
Carbohydrate content: low
Fibre content: low
Protein content: high
Fat content: medium

2 lb (900 g) cod fillet
butter for greasing
grated rind and juice 1 lemon
one 10 oz (275 g) jar mixed pepper antipasto
4 tablespoons chopped parsley
1 teaspoon paprika
¼ teaspoon cayenne pepper
2 small eggs, beaten
1½ oz (40 g) plain flour
salt
freshly-ground black pepper
3 fl oz (90 ml) olive oil
sauce:
12 oz (350 g) tomatoes
1 oz (25 g) butter
1 tablespoon plain flour
1 teaspoon paprika
¼ teaspoon cayenne pepper
½ pint (275 ml) stock (see below)
2 teaspoons tomato purée
bouquet garni

Heat the oven to 350F/180C/gas 4. Skin the cod (page 4). Cut it into pieces about 3 inches (7.5 cm) wide and lay the pieces in a buttered, oven-proof dish. Pour the lemon juice over the top and put the fish into the oven for 30 minutes, or until it is cooked through. Take it out and cool it.

To make the sauce, quarter the tomatoes. Put the butter, flour, paprika, cayenne pepper and stock into a saucepan. Set them on a low to medium heat and bring them to the boil, stirring.

Put in the tomatoes, tomato purée and bouquet garni. Simmer, uncovered, for 25 minutes. Strain the sauce through a sieve, pressing down hard with a wooden spoon to extract as much juice and tomato flesh as possible. Return the sauce to the rinsed pan and simmer it gently for 5 minutes so it becomes thick and smooth.

Flake the fish and put it into a bowl. Chop enough of the antipasto to make 4 tablespoons. Add it to the cod together with the lemon rind, parsley, paprika and cayenne pepper. Beat in the eggs. Put the flour onto a plate and season it. Form the mixture into eight patties. It will be very moist at this stage so spoon each portion onto the plate of flour, form it into a round and turn it over with a fish slice to make sure that it is coated on both sides.

When you have made enough patties to fill your frying pan, heat 3 tablespoons of the oil in the pan and transfer the patties to it, again using the fish slice or palette knife. Cook the patties until they are golden-coloured on both sides and the egg binding them together has set. Remove them and keep them warm. Form the rest of the mixture into patties and cook them in the same way.

To serve, put a portion of the sauce onto each of four dinner plates. Set the patties on top and put a small portion of the antipasto on top of each one.

Chef's tips:

☆ No other garnish is necessary

☆ Serve with a green salad or with lightly-cooked green vegetables; and sauté potatoes, potato slices cut into rings and cooked in the oven in oil and butter, or with new potatoes tossed with butter and parsley.

☆ For the stock use either a home-made vegetable stock or a good quality tomato or vegetable stock cube.

☆ Antipasto is sold in jars to be served as a first course or salad before a main meal of pasta. It consists usually of cooked vegetables, sliced or diced, and placed in an olive oil-based dressing. Sweet pepper antipasto is made from a mixture of red, green and yellow peppers, cut into thin strips.

☆ To serve as a first course, halve all ingredients and make 4 patties.

SPECIAL BROWN RICE PAELLA

Serves: 4
Type of dish: hot main course
Suitable for first course: no
Preparation start time: 1¾ hours before serving
Preparation time: 45 minutes
Waiting time: nil
Cooking time: 1 hour
Suitable for dinner parties: yes
Special equipment: paella pan or large, heavy frying pan with lid or foil
Suitable for microwave cooking: no
Suitable for pressure cooking: no
Suitable for freezing: no
Calorie content: high
Carbohydrate content: high
Fibre content: high
Protein content: high
Fat content: medium

8 oz (225 g) cod fillet
4 chicken drumsticks
4 oz (125 g) chorizo sausage
4 oz (125 g) prawns in shells
1 medium onion
1 garlic clove
pinch salt
1 red pepper
1 green pepper
8 oz (225 g) tomatoes
4 tablespoons olive oil
2 teaspoons paprika
¼ teaspoon cayenne pepper
8 oz (225 g) long grain brown rice
¼ teaspoon saffron soaked in 2 tablespoons boiling water
1 pint (550 ml) chicken stock
12 pimento-stuffed green olives

Skin the cod fillet and cut it into ¾ inch (2 cm) dice. Cut the chorizo sausage into ¼ inch (6 mm) thick slices.

Thinly slice the onion. Crush the garlic with the salt. Core and seed the peppers and cut them into strips. Put the tomatoes into a bowl, pour boiling water over them and leave them for 2 minutes. Drain them and skin them.

Heat the oil in a large, heavy frying pan on a medium heat. Put in the chicken drumsticks and brown them on all sides. Remove them. Put in the slices of sausage and cook them for 2 minutes, turning several times. Remove them.

Lower the heat. Put in the onion and garlic and cook them for 2 minutes. Put in the peppers

and cook for 2 minutes more. Stir in the rice, paprika and cayenne pepper. Pour in the stock and bring it to the boil. Add the saffron and replace the chicken drumsticks and sausage. Cover the pan with a lid or with a large sheet of foil and simmer the paella for 30 minutes. Put in the cod, prawns (in their shells), tomatoes and olives. Cook for a further 10 minutes, or until the rice is cooked and most of the liquid absorbed.

☆　　☆　　☆

Chef's tips:
☆ Serve garnished with lemon wedges.
☆ No accompaniment is necessary but a green salad goes well.

COD AND PRAWN TART

Serves: 4

Type of dish: hot or cold main course

Suitable for first course: yes, see below

Preparation time: 45 minutes

Waiting time: nil

Cooking time: 25 minutes

Suitable for dinner parties: yes and buffet parties

Special equipment: 10 inch (25 cm) diameter tart tin; oven

Suitable for microwave cooking: yes, initial cooking of cod

Suitable for pressure cooking: yes, initial cooking of cod

Suitable for freezing: no

Calorie content: high

Carbohydrate content: medium

Fibre content: low

Protein content: high

Fat content: medium

pastry:
6 oz (175 g) plain flour
pinch salt
3 oz (75 g) butter
cold water to mix
filling:
12 oz (350 g) cod fillet
½ pint (275 ml) milk
1 bay leaf
1 blade mace
1 teaspoon black peppercorns
1 oz (25 g) butter
2 tablespoons plain flour
4 tablespoons chopped parsley
3 oz (75 g) Cheddar cheese, grated
4 oz (125 g) peeled prawns
2 tomatoes

For the pastry, put the flour and salt into a bowl and rub in the butter. Mix to a dough with cold water. Leave the dough in a cool place while you prepare the filling.

Heat the oven to 375F/190C/gas 5. Put the cod fillet into a saucepan with the milk, bay leaf, mace and peppercorns. Bring it gently to the boil and simmer for about 4 minutes, or until it is cooked through. Lift out the cod. Skin and flake it.

Strain and reserve the milk. Put it into a saucepan with the butter and flour. Set it on a medium heat and stir until it boils and you have a thick sauce. Take the pan from the heat. Beat in the parsley and the cheese and fold in the prawns, taking care not to break them up. Fold in the flaked cod. Cool the mixture slightly.

Roll out the pastry and use it to line a 10 inch (25 cm) diameter tart tin. Put in the filling. Cut the tomatoes into rings and arrange them on the top.

Bake the tart for 25 minutes, or until the pastry is cooked through and the top of the filling is beginning to brown.

Serve hot or cold.

Chef's tips:

☆ When the tart is served hot, no additional garnish is necessary. When it is cold, garnish with small parsley sprigs.

☆ Jacket potatoes and a salad are ideal accompaniments whether the tart is to be served hot or cold. Lightly-cooked green vegetables such as peas, green beans or broccoli are also suitable, as are grilled tomato halves.

☆ To serve as a first course, cut the tart into small wedges and serve with a small portion of attractive salad leaves.

FISHERMAN'S PIES

Serves: 4
Type of dish: hot main course
Suitable for first course: no
Preparation start time: 1½ hours before serving
Preparation time: 1 hour
Waiting time: nil
Cooking time: 20 minutes
Suitable for dinner parties: yes
Special equipment: four individual pie dishes
Suitable for microwave cooking: fish can be
   initially cooked in microwave
Suitable for pressure cooking: no
Suitable for freezing: no
Calorie content: high
Carbohydrate content: medium
Fibre content: medium
Protein content: high
Fat content: medium

4 frozen cod steaks
juice ½ lemon
salt
freshly-ground black pepper
3 oz (75 g) butter
1½ lb (675 g) potatoes
3 fl oz (90 ml) milk
8 oz (225 g) runner or French beans
one 12 oz (350 g) can sweetcorn kernels
½ pint (275 ml) vegetable or fish stock (see below)
2 tablespoons plain flour
4 tablespoons chopped parsley
4 tablespoons double cream

Heat the oven to 350F/180C/gas 4. Put the frozen cod steaks into an ovenproof dish. Sprinkle them with lemon juice, season them with salt and pepper and dot them with 1 oz (25 g) of the butter. Cover them with foil or baking parchment and put them into the oven for 15 minutes or until they are cooked through. Lift out the cod steaks and flake them. Reserve the cooking juices. Heat the oven to 400F/200C/gas 6.

Peel the potatoes and boil them in lightly salted water until they are tender. Drain them and mash them with 1 oz (25 g) butter and the milk.

Thinly slice the runner beans or cut the French beans into 1 inch (2.5 cm) lengths. Boil them in lightly-salted water until they are tender. Drain them. Drain the sweetcorn kernels.

Put the stock into a saucepan with the remaining butter and the flour. Set them on a medium heat and stir until they boil and you have a thick

 77

sauce. Stir in the reserved cooking juices. Off the heat, stir in the cream. Fold in the fish, beans, sweetcorn and parsley.

Divide the mixture between four individual pie dishes. Put a portion of the mashed potato on top and make patterns in it with a fork.

Put the pies onto a baking sheet and put them into the oven for 20 minutes, or until the tops have browned.

Place each dish on a dinner plate to serve.

Chef's tips:

☆ Parsley sprigs make the best garnish.
☆ Serve with a green salad which can be either put onto the plate or into a bowl on the side.
☆ For stock, use either a home-made vegetable or fish stock, or good quality stock cubes of the same flavours.

SMOKED COD AND POTATO BAKE

Serves: 4
Type of dish: hot main course
Suitable for first course: no
Preparation time: 1 hour
Waiting time: nil
Cooking time: 25 minutes
Suitable for dinner parties: no
Special equipment: large, shallow, ovenproof dish; steamer
Suitable for microwave cooking: fish can be cooked initially in microwave
Suitable for pressure cooking: no
Suitable for freezing: no
Calorie content: medium
Carbohydrate content: medium
Fibre content: medium
Protein content: high
Fat content: medium

1 lb (450 g) smoked cod
1½ lb (675 g) potatoes
2 green peppers
1 medium onion
1 oz (25 g) butter
½ pint (275 ml) milk
1 bay leaf
1 slice onion
1 blade mace, if available
1 teaspoon black peppercorns
4 tablespoons chopped parsley
4 eggs

Heat the oven to 400F/200C/gas 6. Scrub the
potatoes but do not peel them. Cut them into ¾
inch (2 cm) dice. Put them into a steamer and
place them over a pan of boiling water. Steam
them for 25 minutes, or until they are just tender.

Core and seed the peppers and cut them into
1 inch (2.5 cm) strips. Thinly slice the onion.

Melt the butter in a saucepan on a low heat.
Put in the onion and cook it for 2 minutes. Put
in the peppers, cover and cook gently for 10
minutes.

Skin the fish. Put it into a saucepan with the
milk, bay leaf, onion slice, blade of mace and
peppercorns. Cover and set it on a low heat.
Bring the milk to the boil and then gently poach
the fish for 2 minutes, or until it is just cooked
through. Lift out the fish. Strain and reserve the
milk.

Flake the fish. In a bowl, mix it with the potatoes, onion and peppers and parsley. Put the fish and vegetables into a shallow, ovenproof dish.

Beat the eggs and beat in the reserved milk. Pour the mixture over the fish and potatoes.

Put the dish into the oven for 25 minutes, or until the custard mixture is set and the top is just beginning to brown.

Chef's tips:
☆ Serve straight from the dish.
☆ Lightly-cooked green vegetables, such as peas, broccoli, green beans or cauliflower are the best accompaniment. A green salad is also suitable.
☆ Mace: see glossary (page 12).

SMOKED COD KEDGEREE

Serves: 4
Type of dish: hot main course
Suitable for first course: no
Preparation start time: 1½ hours before serving
Preparation time: 30 minutes
Waiting time: nil
1st cooking time: 40 minutes rice; 5 minutes fish
2nd cooking time: 20 minutes (finished dish)
Suitable for dinner parties: no
Special equipment: large, heavy frying pan
Suitable for microwave cooking: cod and/or rice
　　can be cooked initially in microwave
Suitable for pressure cooking: no
Suitable for freezing: yes, see below
Calorie content: medium
Carbohydrate content: high
Fibre content: high
Protein content: high
Fat content: medium

10 oz (275 g) long grain brown rice
½ teaspoon salt
1½ lb (675 g) smoked cod
¼ pint (150 ml) milk
1 bayleaf
½ teaspoon black peppercorns
1 blade mace
1 large onion
6 oz (175 g) shelled peas, fresh or frozen
4 oz (125 g) peanuts
2 oz (50 g) raisins
2 teaspoons Madras curry powder
1 teaspoon ground turmeric
¼ pint (150 ml) thick, full cream yoghurt
1 teaspoon lime pickle

Put the rice into a saucepan with 1¼ pints (725 ml) water and the salt. Bring it to the boil, cover and simmer for 40 minutes or until the rice is tender and all the water absorbed.

Skin the cod (page 4). Put it into a shallow saucepan with the milk and enough water to cover. Add the bayleaf, peppercorns and mace.

Thinly slice the onion and add one slice to the pan. Cover the fish and put it on top of the stove on a medium heat. Bring it to the boil and simmer for 2 minutes or until it is cooked through. Lift it out. Skin and flake it.

Cook the peas in boiling water for 5 minutes. Drain them.

Heat the oil in a large frying pan on a low heat. Put in the onion and soften it. Mix in the rice, fish, peas, peanuts and raisins. Scatter in

the curry powder and turmeric and toss all the ingredients together on the heat until they are well mixed and have become an even yellow colour.

Put the kedgeree onto a flat serving dish. Chop any large pieces in the lime pickle and mix the pickle into the yoghurt. Spoon the yoghurt down the centre of the kedgeree.

☆　　☆　　☆

Chef's tips:

☆ Garnish with coriander or parsley sprigs if wished.

☆ Serve with a green salad. No other accompaniment is necessary.

☆ White rice can be used instead of brown, in which case, use the same amount of water and salt but reduce the cooking time to 15 - 20 minutes.

☆ To freeze, cool the kedgeree completely. Do not add the yoghurt and pickle. Pack the kedgeree into a rigid plastic container and cover it. Store it for up to one month. Thaw in the refrigerator. To reheat, melt 1 oz (25 g) butter in a large, heavy frying pan on a medium heat. Stir the kedgeree in the butter until it has heated through.

☆ Mace: see glossary (page 12).

☆ Turmeric: see glossary (page 12).

SMOKED COD AND FRENCH BEAN SALAD

Serves: 4
Type of dish: cold main course
Suitable for first course: yes, see below
Preparation start time: 4½ hours before serving
Preparation time: 45 minutes
Waiting time: 4 hours (overlaps with preparation time
Cooking time: 10 minutes
Suitable for dinner parties: buffet parties
Special equipment: shallow saucepan
Suitable for microwave cooking: yes, fish and beans can be cooked initially in microwave
Suitable for pressure cooking: yes, fish and beans can be cooked initially in pressure cooker
Suitable for freezing: no
Calorie content: medium
Carbohydrate content: low
Fibre content: low
Protein content: high
Fat content: medium

1½ lb (675 g) smoked cod fillet
bouquet garni
1 blade mace
1 teaspoon black peppercorns
1 slice of onion
8 oz (225 g) thin French beans
6 spring onions
¼ pint (150 ml) milk
1 lettuce
4 tomatoes
½ cucumber
dressing:
1 lemon
4 tablespoons olive oil
1 tablespoon white wine vinegar
1 tablespoon chopped thyme, or ½ teaspoon dried
1 tablespoon chopped tarragon, or ½ teaspoon dried
1 tablespoon chopped marjoram, or ½ teaspoon dried
1 tablespoon chopped fennel
1 garlic clove, crushed with pinch salt
freshly-ground black pepper

First make the *dressing*. Cut the rind and pith from the lemon and thinly slice the flesh. Beat the oil and vinegar with the herbs, garlic and pepper. Add the pieces of lemon and let the dressing stand for 4 hours at room temperature.

Put the fish into a shallow pan with the bouquet garni, mace, peppercorns and onion slice. Pour in the milk and then enough water to just

 87

cover the fish. Bring the fish to the boil and simmer it gently for 5 minutes, or until it is just cooked through. Lift it out, flake it, remove the skin and bones and let it cool.

Top and tail the beans and cut them into lengths of about 1½ inches (4 cm). Cook them in lightly-salted boiling water for 5 minutes. Drain and cool them. Finely chop the spring onions.

To finish the dressing, press down hard on the lemon slices to extract as much juice from them as possible. Then discard them.

In a bowl, mix the fish with the beans and spring onions. Fold in the dressing.